MAURI ORA

WISDOM FROM THE MĀORI WORLD

MAURI ORA

WISDOM FROM THE MĀORI WORLD

**PETER ALSOP &
TE RAU KUPENGA**

pb potton & burton

Ka tuku tēnei pukapuka hei tohu whakamaharatanga
ki tō māua pāpā, a Dr Apirana Tuahae Mahuika.
Ka mau tonu māua ki āna kōrero, āna tohutohu me tana
aroha hei korowai tauawhi mō ngā rā kei te heke mai.

'E hara taku maunga a Hikurangi i te maunga
haere. He maunga tu tonu. Ko tōku mana nō
tuawhakarere no te ihu tō mai te pō.'

We dedicate this book to our Uncle and Papa,
Dr Apirana Tuahae Mahuika.
We will forever hold fast to his wisdom,
guidance and love as a precious gift.

'My mountain Hikurangi does not move. It has
remained steadfast since the shades of creation
conferring on me my absolute sovereignty.'

First published in 2016 by Potton & Burton

Potton & Burton
98 Vickerman Street, PO Box 5128, Nelson, New Zealand
pottonandburton.co.nz

Text © Peter Alsop & Te Rau Kupenga
Design – The Gas Project

Previous page: Dr Apirana Mahuika, 2014
Image courtesy of Te Rūnanganui ō Ngāti Porou

ISBN 978 0 947503 14 7

Printed in China by Midas Printing International Ltd

CONTENTS

INTRODUCTION PETER ALSOP

After a great childhood in Rotorua, my working life in Wellington led to meeting
Airihi Mahuika, daughter of Poihipi/Bussy (1925–2004), and a connection to the
people of Ngāti Porou. We were married by Apirana/Uncle Api (1934–2015), a man
who symbolised wisdom to me, in St Mary's Church, Tikitiki. That's a special
place; a majestic memorial to the Maori Batallion, built on the instigation of
Sir Apirana Ngata (1874–1950), one of New Zealand's greatest leaders.

Reflecting back, Uncle Api was a key inspiration for this book. Talking with him,
and hearing his public oratory, was a great inspiration. From a position of deep
knowledge, he was expansive in his vision; engaging with his stories; generous
with his warmth; and he had an unparalleled eloquence with words.

Around the time I met Uncle Api, I exhibited a series of typographical paintings
of whakataukī (proverbs). I was fascinated by their metaphoric property, full of
insightful life lessons. I enjoyed the incongruity of simplicity and substance.
And I liked the productivity of words; their ability to engender contemplation
far deeper than the pithy phrase on a page.

For that exhibition, I wrote that 'the lessons stand out, like white on black, as
virtues of a life well-lived'. Here, six virtues are used to structure the book, a
robust recipe for personal satisfaction drawn from the field of positive psychology.
Inspired by the pages ahead, it's our hope that your personal leadership and
fulfilment, in whatever setting, will reach new heights.

My warm thanks go to Te Rau for his friendship and partnership in this project;
to Gary Stewart for his leadership of book design; and – importantly – to all the
people, past and present, associated with the whakataukī and images.

Thank you for your interest in the kaupapa (topic). Best wishes for the future;
herein lies some powerful wisdom to make it even better.

TĪMATATANGA TE RAU KUPENGA

E ngā tini whanaunga, e ngā hoa, tēnā koutou, kia ora tātau i roto i ngā āhuatanga o te wā e papaki nei i a tātau. Tangihia o tātau mate. Rātau i kapohia e te ringa kaha o aituā. No reira, tukuna rātau ki te pō, taka iho ki a tātau ngā waihotanga iho a rātau mā, tēnā ano tātau katoa. Heoi, kei te Runga Rawa ngā manaakitanga me te whakapakaritanga mā tātau.

I remember as a boy talking with my mother, who fostered in me a love of oral history, and asking her the meaning of a particular saying. Her response was 'what does it mean to you?' She followed up with 'take what is meant for you, and leave the rest for others'. That, in essence, is how I define the purpose of this book. We are offering the wisdom of our ancestors to guide a better future.

I was privileged to be born into a whānau (family) and iwi (tribe) with a cultural identity founded on rich oral history. Our tribal leaders were some of the greatest proponents of Māori language and culture. These women and men were exceptional leaders of preserving knowledge, and using it to influence our decisions today.

I will be forever grateful to my Papa, Apirana Mahuika, for his generosity of heart and spirit in sharing his world with me. I was honoured to spend many a day driving my Pāpā to tribal gatherings; sitting with him around the kitchen table; and observing him in action in meetings and on the marae. He challenged me with a critical and enquiring mind. He growled at me to teach valuable life lessons. He exposed me to a style of leadership and personal brilliance that has helped shape me and my decision-making today. Most importantly, he and my nanny Karin loved me unconditionally, generously and wholeheartedly.

Papa is the inspiration for this book. I'm grateful to Peter that, through our mutual love and admiration for this remarkable man, we can dedicate this book to his memory. Kia ora.

TIRO WHĀNUI
OVERVIEW

TIRO WHĀNUI OVERVIEW

It is said that if you want to know a culture, know their proverbs. That's a proverb in itself. Yet it's also an unlikely starting point for cultural learning in the information-overload world of now. Therein lies the purpose of this book: to share the gifts of cultural knowledge to new audiences in a new and engaging way.

In Aotearoa New Zealand, indigenous culture – the world of Māori – is founded on a rich tradition of oral history. Māori have always been great developers and sharers of knowledge, galvanised for centuries in proverbs, or whakataukī. There is a wealth of knowledge, long on meaning and significance but, importantly, short enough to remember and pass on.

In many ways, that is the point of whakataukī: a speedy look to the past to help forge the future. Whakataukī are drawn from the accumulated experience of a culture; a gift from the school of life, distilled to its most potent form, to catapult new generations to higher wellbeing. They provide meaning and help make sense of the world; a road-map for living harmoniously with others, and for successfully manoeuvring through the environment of the day. They're a vehicle for conveying a values system and, above all else, ingredients for living a great life.

The enduring power of story

Wisdom is universal and is not confined by generations, by oceans or by cultures. It is part of the legacy of humankind.[1] – Sir Hirini Moko Mead

From the Bible to Aesop's Fables, proverbs go back a long time, as does the study of proverbs called 'paremiology'. Notwithstanding, there's no single definition of what is and what isn't a proverb. Definitions range from 'the wit of one and the wisdom of many' (Lord John Russell in the 1850s); 'an incommunicable quality' (Archer Taylor, 1931); to longer versions like 'a short, generally known sentence of the folk which contains wisdom, truth, morals, and traditional views in a metaphorical, fixed, and memorisable form and which is handed down from generation to generation' (Wolfgang Meider, 1993).

There are appealing qualities to all these definitions, but there's something much richer in their combined effect. Together, they paint a picture of the gravitas of proverbs, combining simplicity and complexity. It's a communication form that people seem to intuitively know; an innate definition that starts being 'written' in childhood and thereafter refined through life. The formula goes something like this: People are naturally interested in stories. Stories are memorable. Story upon story, people build a story of what's a good story. The most concise and insightful stories are proverbs.

The power of proverbs can also depend on how the story is told. The best story-tellers know the power of connection, whether that be the spoken word or, as part of this book, the use of imagery. An expert can engage and hold an audience, captivating emotions through language, humour, empathy, projection, timing, anecdote and even innuendo. Senses are aroused. It's often a rich cocktail of cerebral and emotional responses; you know it when you feel it. For centuries across cultures, people have marvelled at the ability of those who are best, yet struggled to neatly define the secret sauce and, harder still, apply it to good personal effect.

The place of whakataukī

Māori have generated and celebrated a large number of amazing story-tellers over time. This is unsurprising for a culture steeped in oral history, within which the art of oral history is oratory. The ability to take a historical lesson, clothed within a whakataukī and adapted to a contemporary setting, has been the talent of Māori oratory masters through time.

Practically speaking, an upbringing in and around Māori practices, including marae-based events at which oratory is a central feature, sets the scene for oral history and story-telling as key planks of life. In its prime, there is an innate ability to connect with people; across iwi (tribal affiliations), across generations and even across kaupapa (work or focus areas). Both celebration and mourning bring out the best; speaker after speaker elevating the meaning and significance of events to high levels of remembrance.

The dedication of this book to Dr Apirana Mahuika (1934–2015) is, alongside whānau (family) connections, a recognition of his standing within the Māori world and wider society for insightful commentary and impactful ability with words. A gifted orator and tribal leader, he often conveyed messages through story, relayed through an analogous historic event, a waiata (song), quote or whakataukī. And there was typically a very strong point.

A special aspect of whakataukī to Māori culture is the reverberation of an ancestral voice, one of Mahuika's speaking specialities. At a gathering in Ruatoria, for example, a doubting comment was made about the suitability of a humble elder to sit on a governance board. Mahuika's response was 'ahakoa tana kōtahi, he manomano kei muri' (while she is but one, she represents a multitude). This statement related to an ancestress, Hinetapora, an exceptional leader in her time. A war lord from a neighbouring tribe waged war on Hinetapora and took her life. The event has been captured for centuries in the whakataukī, denoting the importance of never underestimating one's opponent. In context, the doubting comment also related to a descendant of Hinetapora, with Mahuika's response reflecting the importance of female leadership within his tribe, Ngāti Porou.

Every iwi and hapū (sub-tribe) around Aotearoa have similar examples to share; stories and proverbs that have survived and been repeatedly passed on. The examples are extremely diverse but, with a common tradition of oral history, share a central unifying theme. That is, a connection with the voices, minds and experiences of ancestors. Or, as beautifully spoken by Sir Hirini Moko Mead, a notable academic and Ngāti Awa leader, whakataukī constitute 'a communication with ancestors ... their advice is as valuable today as before ... their use of metaphor and their economy of words become a beautiful legacy to pass on to generations yet unborn. In a sense it is a rare privilege to be able to reach out to the ancestors and touch their minds.'[2] In that sense, whakataukī embody respect and, by gifting past knowledge forward, they are treasures that appreciate with time.

This book's approach

E tipu, e rea, mō ngā rā o tōu ao,
ko tō ringa ki ngā rākau ā te Pākehā hei ōranga mō tō tinana,
kō tō ngākau ki ngā tāonga ā ō tīpuna Māori hei tikitiki mō tō māhunga,
ā kō tō wairua ki tō Atua, nāna nei ngā mea katoa.

Grow up o tender youth and thrive in the days destined for you,
your hand to the tools of the Pākehā to provide physical sustenance,
your heart to the treasures of your ancestors to adorn your head,
your soul to God to whom all things belong.
– Sir Apirana Ngata, 1874–1950

In 1949, just before his death, Sir Apirana Ngata wrote 'E Tipu E Rea'. One of Aotearoa's greatest leaders, Ngata wrote the poem for his mokopuna (grandchild), setting out a framework for her to live a balanced life. Nearly 70 years on, the framework still rings true, timeless in both meaning and motivation.

Ngata's wisdom was a guiding light for this book and, to honour his holistic aspiration, led to the use of a framework developed by Martin Seligman, a professor of psychology at the University of Pennsylvania. Seligman is heralded as the father of positive psychology, a momentous contribution to humanity given the field's focus on understanding and building human happiness.

Seligman's key finding for this book – a finding replicated and validated across cultures and time – is that the deployment of six 'humanist ideals of virtue' is central to happiness and wellbeing. And, for maximum effect, that these virtues are deployed for 'meaning and purpose', essentially for greater good, and not just for 'pleasure and gratification' (as important as they are too).[3] To quote Seligman: 'Positive psychology takes you through the countryside of pleasure and gratification, up into the high country of strength and virtue, and finally to the peaks of lasting fulfillment: meaning and purpose. ... Use your signature strengths and virtues in the service of something much larger than you.'

And that, fundamentally, is what whakataukī are all about. In the pursuit of maximising wellbeing, whakataukī guide the way, for individuals, families, communities and organisations. From high moral standards come higher standards, building greater social capital than would otherwise have been the case. It's a virtuous cycle for harmony and wellbeing we all have the option to pursue.

The virtues

The six virtues adopted for this book – the overall structure for grouping whakataukī – are introduced below. Some virtues have been labelled slightly

differently to Seligman's choices, though importantly the substance of his preeminent work is preserved.

Mātauranga/Wisdom – Wisdom is the ability to apply experience, knowledge and judgement to enlighten and assist a situation. There is something especially meaningful in being with a wise person; often generating life-long memories from sage or insightful comments and/or the manner in which those comments were conveyed. The Māori term 'mātauranga' literally means to enlighten or illuminate. Within the Māori world, wisdom doesn't necessarily equate to age, though experience plays a major part, along with humility.

Māia/Courage – Māori oral history is filled with examples of the courageous spirit of ancestors; their ability to stare down adversity and draw on strength in the face of pain, grief or challenge. The courageous Māori heart was demonstrated in World War II with the formation of the 28th Maori Battalion; the Companies selected along tribal lines while kinship connected them all. Whakataukī would have been, for some, the last words heard on New Zealand soil: 'Kia māia tō tū, kia pakari tō tū, kia Māori tō tū' (Be courageous, be strong, be Māori). There is much to be said for that message in any culture and in facing any type of challenge: in essence, what is honoured most is that you give your best and you are yourself.

Atawhai/Compassion – While compassion can involve being aware of, and being sympathetic towards, another's suffering, the concept of atawhai is much deeper. Atawhai evokes different emotions depending on the situation, environment and context. Atawhai is expressed powerfully during tangi (bereavement process) but it can also be shown through affection, caring advice, kindness and benevolence, as well as romantic love.

Ngākau tapatahi/Integrity – At times on the marae, when children are being naughty or people are not listening, an elder might say, 'kia tika ō mahi' (do what is right). The term ngākau tapatahi builds on the concepts of tika (proper and fair) and pono (truth and sincerity), by adding an overarching expectation of ethical and moral conduct. The high relevance of tika and pono to integrity is well-illustrated by the mission statement that Mahuika developed for the New Zealand Independent Police Conduct Authority: 'Whāia te pono, kia puawai ko te tika' (Seek out the truth, that justice may prevail).

Whakahautanga/Self-mastery – Aristotle said that 'knowing yourself is the beginning of all wisdom'; a proverb that underscores the interdependency of wisdom and self-mastery (and, in fact, the chemistry between all virtues in this book). Self-mastery is particularly important; the ability to modify behaviour and actions for desirable effect. Even when it comes to personal strengths, there's a well-known saying that every strength overused or misused becomes a weakness. Self-mastery is a complex art that can never really be perfected.

Whakapono/Belief – A fundamental aspect of the Māori world view is belief; an acceptance that something exists beyond physical reality. An acknowledgement of the spiritual realm is a feature in most, if not all, Māori cultural rituals. All rituals on a marae normally acknowledge this realm, from the karanga (call of welcome) to visitors coming on to a marae, the whaikōrero (the speeches/oratory), the karakia (prayer) and the poroporoāki (farewell). Belief is demonstrated by acknowledging family and friends who are no longer present in the physical realm; by recognising the spiritual deities; and seeking, and being grateful for, spiritual protection.

The whakataukī and images

The choice of specific whakataukī for this book has been hard. In particular, narrowing the selection field has been challenging, as has deciding the right mix for a balanced book seeking cross-cultural appeal. Central to selection has been a desire to reflect, through individual whakataukī, the components or 'traits' of each virtue, such as the different forms and aspects of courage that, together, embody its full meaning and effect.

Once the traits and whakataukī were settled, appropriate images were married in. A strong literary and visual union was the aim, in the hope of creating a memorable multi-sensory experience. The selection process also included careful consideration of cultural appropriateness, far beyond European conventions of copyright and permissions, to think of iwi, hapū and whānau perspectives of seeing ancestors or important cultural events in print.

The creation and presentation of the material as a trilogy – a trait, whakataukī and an image – was also influenced by the three kete (baskets) of knowledge: *te kete aronui* – the basket that contains the knowledge of what we see (the image); *te kete tuauri* – the basket containing the understanding of the physical world (the trait, being what is or isn't displayed by a person here and now); and *te kete tuatea* – the basket containing knowledge beyond space and time (the whakataukī, drawing on timeless traditional knowledge for current and future use).

Applying the knowledge

A kete in the Māori world is also synonymous with a basket of choice; a choice of what contents go in and get taken out and, once removed, how they are used for best effect. In that sense, the book presents options and invitations; a whakataukī menu waiting for the right occasion, time or place.

There are some aspects of this book that will invariably attract different interpretations and opinions and, accepting subjectivity, the book should be seen as a guide. Wellbeing is a complex concept, defined in the eye of the beholder. People will have different views on the virtues, traits and translations but, beyond detailed debates, the concepts and intent are likely to stand strong.

To paraphrase Aristotle, the ultimate in wellbeing is to know oneself. Fundamental to knowing oneself, is to know one's place in the world. Beyond the individual, in the Māori world that relates to connection with others, the environment and with the spiritual realm. The usual way of finding answers is to return home to tribal land, back to familiar landmarks to see familiar people and spend comforting time on a familiar marae. 'E hoki ki ō maunga, ki ō awa, kia purea ai koe i ngā hauora ō Tāwhirimātea' (Return to your mountains, and to your rivers, that you may be cleansed by the healing winds of Tāwhirimatea, the god of weather).

The contents of this book help crystallise and illustrate these important connections, with the offer that this traditional Māori knowledge has both contemporary and cross-cultural appeal. We wish you well on your life journey. We hope there's something valuable here to help you on your way.

CHAPTER 1

MĀTAURANGA
WISDOM

MĀTANGA
EXPERIENCED

E kore e mau i a koe,
he wae kai pakiaka

You will not catch the feet
accustomed to running
among the roots

WHAKAARO WHĀNUI
BROAD-MINDED

He rangi tā matawhāiti,
he rangi tā matawhānui

A person with narrow vision
has a restricted horizon;
a person with wide vision
has plentiful opportunities

PŪMAHARA
SAVVY

E kore te pātiki e hoki ki tōna puehu

The flounder does not return to its dust

HŌHONUTANGA
DEPTH

**He kino ra, he kino
nō tāu ō te wai**

I may not be good-looking
but I am the deepest
part of the river

MŌHIOTANGA
INSIGHTFUL

He tangata kī tahi

A person of a single word

MATATAU
DISCERNING

He ika paewai anake hei
tomo i roto i te hīnaki

Nothing but eels
enter my eel pot

MATAKITE
FORESIGHT

Ka whāia te wāhie
mo takurua ka mahia
te kai mō te tau

If you look for firewood
in the winter, you will
have plenty of food
all year round

TŪTURU
WELL-ROUNDED

**Tangata ako ana i
te kāenga, te tūranga ki
te marae, tau ana**

A person nurtured in the
community contributes
strongly to society

TOHUNGATANGA
LEARNED

Ko te kai a te rangatira he kōrero

The food of chiefs is dialogue

WHAKATIPURANGA
SUCCESSION

**Māku te ra e tō ana;
kei a koe te urunga ake o te rā**

Let mine be the setting sun;
yours is the dawning of a new day

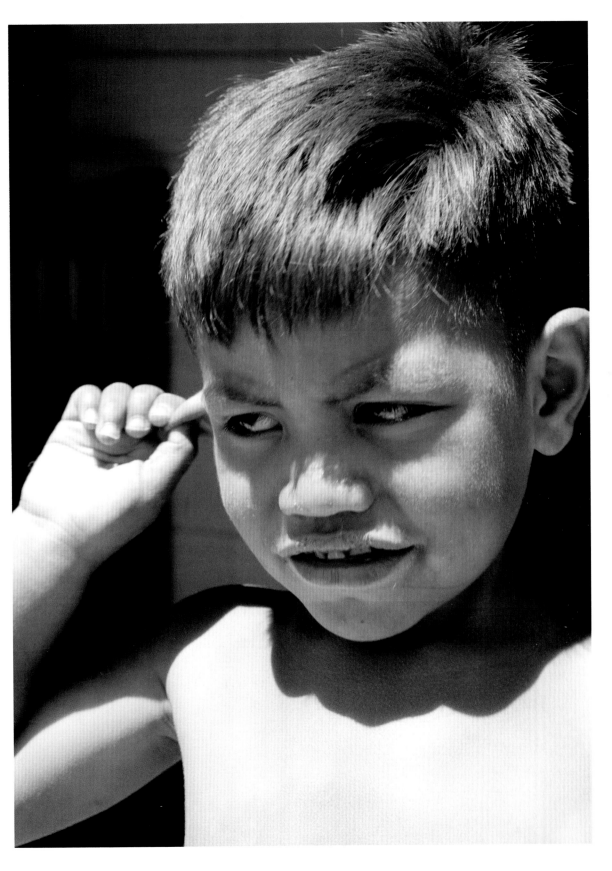

CHAPTER 2

MĀIA

COURAGE

PĀKAHA
BOLDNESS

Iti te matakahi, pangāia
ki te tōtara pakaru ai

The wedge may be small
but it will split the
greatest tōtara

KORONGA
PURPOSE

He manako te kōura i kore ai

Wishing for the crayfish won't bring it

PAKARI
RESILIENCE

He toka tū moana

As durable as a rock
pounded by the surf

AMORANGI
LEADERSHIP

Waiho rā kia tū takitahi ana ngā whetū o te rangi

Let it be one alone
that stands among the
other stars in the sky

TŪRANGATIRA
PRESENCE

**Tama tū, tama ora,
tama noho, tama mate**

He who stands, lives;
he who sits, perishes

HAO NUI
AMBITION

He mate kāhu kōrako

Desire the hawk with
white feathers

WHAKAOHO
MOTIVATION

Mauri tū,
mauri ora

An active soul is
a healthy soul

NIWHA
GRIT

**Ka mahi te tawa
uho ki te riri**

Well done, you whose
courage is like the
heart of a tawa tree

TOA
BRAVERY

Kia mate ururoa,
kei mate wheke

Fight like a shark,
not an octopus

MANAWAROA
FORTITUDE

Ko te whare tū ki te koraha
he kai mā te ahi; ko te whare
tū ki te pā tūwatawata
he tohu nō te rangatira

A solitary house will succumb
to fire; a house in the stockaded
pā is a sign of a chief

CHAPTER 3

ATAWHAI

COMPASSION

PUKUAROHA
EMPATHY

Nā koutou i tangi, nā tātau katoa

When you cry, your tears are shed by us all

HOHOU RONGO

FORGIVENESS

Utua te kino
i te pai

**Repay bad deeds
with good**

WHAIWHAKAARO
THOUGHTFULNESS

E iti noa ana,
nā te aroha

Although it is small,
it is given with love

TAUTOKO
SUPPORT

**Waiho i te toipoto,
kaua i te toiroa**

Let us keep close
together, not far apart

PONO
SINCERITY

**Ka rongo i te ia o te aroha,
he ngākau māhaki**

To feel genuine intentions
is to understand
a charitable heart

MANAAKITANGA
KINDNESS

He aroha whakatō,
he aroha ka puta mai

If kindness is sown,
then kindness is what
you shall receive

WHAKATAU
WELCOMING

He waka eke noa

A vehicle upon which
everyone may embark

AROHA
LOVE

**Mā te ngākau
aroha koe e ārahi**

Let a loving heart
guide your decisions

NGĀKAUPAI
POSITIVITY

Me te wai kōrari

Like honey of the flax

NGĀKAUAROHA
SYMPATHY

**Waiho kia tangi ahau
ki taku tūpāpaku;
kāpā he uru tī e pihi ake**

Let me weep for my deceased;
they are not like the head
of a cabbage tree that regrows

CHAPTER 4

NGĀKAU TAPATAHI

INTEGRITY

MAHITIKA
DECENCY

Kia ū ki te pai

Cleave to that which is good

NGAKĀUPONO
FAIRNESS

He kōanga tangata tahi,
he ngāhuru pukahu noa

Scarce at planting,
all present at harvest

MOTUHENGA
AUTHENTICITY

Tohaina ō painga ki te ao

Share your gifts with the world

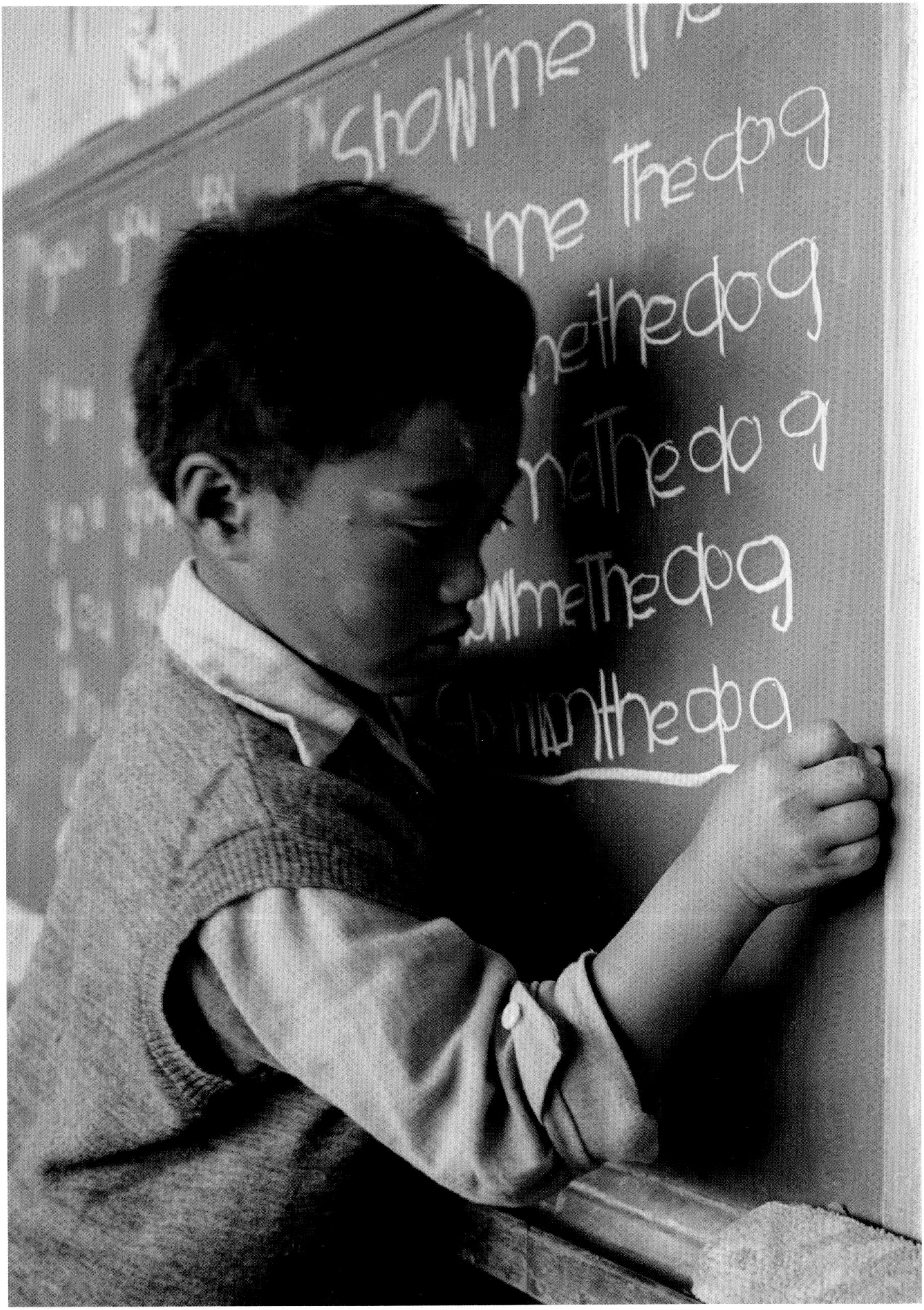

TAKETAKE
GROUNDED

Kia mau ki te aka matua, kei mau ki te aka tāepa

Hold the vine rooted in the ground, not the vine hanging from the heavens

WHAKAMĀNAWA
HONOUR

E kore e hekeheke,
he kākano rangatira

A noble heritage
will never perish

PONONGA
HONESTY

Waiho noa iho ngā taonga, tērā te mana o te rangatira

Leave your belongings anywhere, such is the honesty shown by a leader

PUKUMAHI
HARD WORK

Whakanuia te tangata ringa raupā

Respect a person
with calloused hands

WHAKANUI
RESPECT

He tangata takahi manuhiri, he marae puehu

When a guest is disrespected, the marae suffers

WHAKAAETANGA
ACCEPTANCE

Matua whakapai i
tōhou marae, ka whakapai
ai i te marae o etahi

First set in order
your own courtyard before
you clean up another's

CHAPTER 5

WHAKAHAUTANGA
SELF-MASTERY

AHUMAHI
INDUSTRIOUS

Ko mahi, ko kai;
ko noho, ko iri

Industry is food;
idleness is hunger

TŌTIKA
BALANCE

**Mahia i runga i te rangimārie
me te ngākau māhaki**

With a peaceful mind and
respectful heart, we will
always get the best results

MĀRAMATANGA
PERSPECTIVE

**He pakaru a waka
e taea te raupine mai**

A damaged vehicle
can be repaired

MAHITAHI
COLLABORATION

**E hara taku toa
i te toa takitahi,
he toa takitini**

My strength is not
as an individual,
but as a collective

MĀHAKI
HUMILITY

**Kaore te kūmara e kōrero
mō tōna ake reka**

The sweet potato does not
talk of its sweetness

WHAKAANGA
ENGAGEMENT

He manu aute,
e taea te whakahoro

A kite that is slackened
off flies away

WHAKARITENGA
PREPARATION

Mā roto hoki kia ora
ka pai te kōrero

When refreshed,
the conversation will
be agreeable

WHAKAAROHANGA
CONSIDERATION

Tūtohu ahiahi, whakarere hāpara

Accept in the evening, reject in the morning

WHAKAPŪMAHARA
REFLECTION

Ko te kupu whakahāwea
meinga hei wero
ki te hinengaro

Let belittling words
be a challenge
to the mind

MANAWANUI
PATIENCE

E koa koe aianei,
ā māku hoki tērā apōpō

You rejoice today, but my
turn will come tomorrow

CHAPTER 6

WHAKAPONO

BELIEF

TAUMAURI
PHILOSOPHICAL

**E huri tō aroaro ki te rā,
tukuna tō ataarangi
ki muri i a koe**

Turn and face the sun
and let your shadow fall
behind you

MIHI
GRATITUDE

Pai ake te iti i
te kore rawātu

Little is better than
nothing at all

NGĀKAU MŌHIO
UNDERSTANDING

Tēnā te ngaru whati, tēnā te ngaru puku

There is a wave that breaks, there is a wave that swells

MĪHARO
WONDER

E tūtaki ana ngā kapua
o te rangi, kei runga te
Mangōroa e kōpae pū ana

The clouds in the sky gather,
but above them extends
the Milky Way

MARIU
OPTIMISM

He ua ki te pō,
he paewai ki te ao

Rain at night,
eels at dawn

MANATIAKI
STEWARDSHIP

**Tukua ki tua,
ki ngā rā o te waru e**

Leave it for the future, for
the days when food is scarce

WAWATA
ASPIRATION

Ko te pae tawhiti,
whāia kia tata; ko te pae
tata, whakamaua kia tīna

Seek out distant horizons
and cherish those you attain

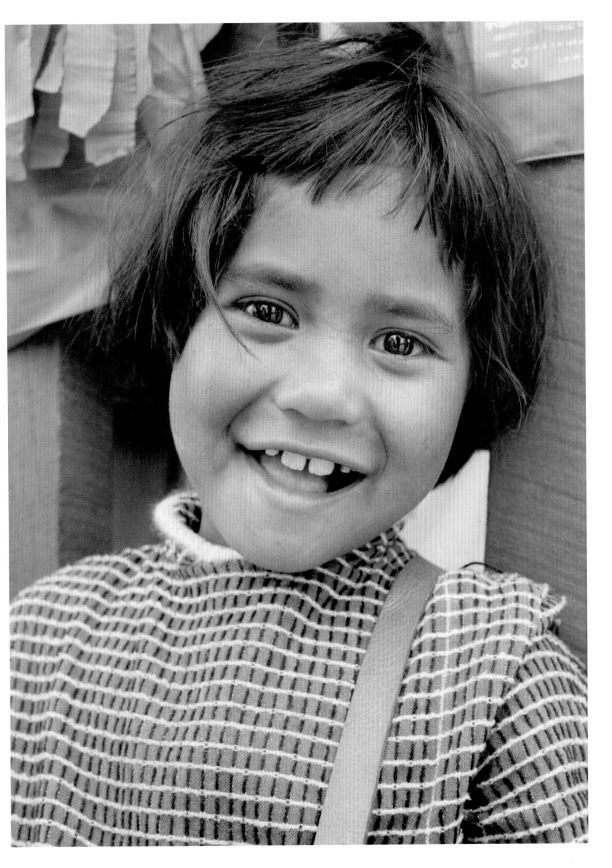

WHAKAHOUANGA
RENEWAL

Mate atu he tētēkura,
ka whakaeke mai he tētēkura

As one frond perishes
another grows in its place

KAITIAKITANGA
GUARDIANSHIP

Toitū te whenua, whatungarongaro he tangata

The land remains when people have disappeared

WHAKAMANAWA
SELF-BELIEF

**He matua pou whare,
e rokohia ana; he matua
tangata, e kore e rokohia**

You can always gain
shelter in your house, but
not always with other people

TŪRANGAWAEWAE
BELONGING

E kore au e ngaro,
he kākano i ruia
mai i Rangiātea

I will never be lost,
for I am a seed
sown in the heavens

TŪMANAKO
HOPE

**Kia mau ki te tūmanako,
te whakapono me te aroha**

Hold fast to hope,
faith and love

KUPU ĀPITI ENDNOTES

ACKNOWLEDGEMENTS

We acknowledge the special contributions made to this book by:

Hone Apanui, for his guidance and wisdom;
Gary Stewart, for his devotion to book design;
Martin Seligman, for permission to use his virtues framework;
Robbie Burton and Alan Bridgland of Potton & Burton for design and production support;
David Alsop, Suite Gallery, for provision of photographs taken by Ans Westra; and
Airihi Mahuika, Fiona Apanui and our tamariki for accommodating our efforts on this project.

OVERVIEW REFERENCES

1. Mead, Hirini Moko, 2003, *Ngā Pēpeha a ngā Tīpuna: The sayings of the ancestors*, Victoria University Press, Wellington, p. 9.
2. Ibid.
3. Seligman, Martin, E.P., 2004, *Character Strengths and Virtues: A handbook and classification*, Oxford University Press, New York and American Psychological Association, Washington, DC.

IMAGE CREDITS

Kei te mihi atu ki te hunga kei roto i ēnei whakaahua me te iwi whaipaanga ki nga whakaahua nei. He ataahua, he taonga katoa. Ka nui te mihi me te aroha.

Alexander Turnbull Library collection: ATL; Ans Westra photographs: Images used courtesy of Suite Gallery. References searchable on the ATL website.

Tiro Whānui – Overview

p. 10: Young Māori woman, Frank Denton, 4 June 1904, ATL, 1/1-020797-G; **p. 12:** Parakino School, Whanganui River, Ans Westra, 1963, AWM-0403-F_05; **p. 17:** Pipiriki, Whanganui River, Ans Westra, 1963, AWM-0261-F_03; **p. 21:** New Generation, Ian McLeod, c.1965, Reproduced with permission of the Photographic Society of New Zealand, Originally published in the Society's 1967 publication *Camera in New Zealand*.

Mātauranga – Wisdom

p. 22: Unidentified man, Northwood Brothers, Date unknown, ATL, 1/1-010678-G; **p. 25:** Kuia carrying young child, Leo White, 1938, ATL, WA-12534-G; **p. 26:** Hare Rakena Te Awe Awe, Photographer unknown, c.1900, Palmerston North City Library, 2013N_Pi150_007389; **p. 29:** Whitebaiting in the Bay of Plenty, Leo White, c.1920-40, ATL, WA-25215-G; **p. 30:** Māori guard and prisoner at the Japanese prisoner of war camp near Featherston, John Pascoe, 1943, ATL, 1/4-000790-F; **p. 33:** Tom Kaua, Welcome for Colombo Plan students, Ruatoria, Ans Westra, May 1963, AWM-0460-F_02; **p. 34:** Eel trap near outlet of Lake Horowhenua, Leslie

Adkin, 1925, Te Papa Tongarewa, B.021666; **p. 37:** Kawhia Harbour, Ans Westra, 1962, AWM-0214-F_11; **p. 38:** Summer Child Studies series, Leo White, 1947, ATL, WA-10160-G; **p. 40:** Annual World War One Maori Servicemen's Reunion, Tikitiki marae, Ans Westra, 1963, AWM-0440-F_09; **p. 43:** Pipiriki, Whanganui River, Ans Westra, 1963, AWM-0263-F_11.

Māia – Courage

p. 44: Personnel of the Maori Battalion with captured enemy material near Gazala, Libya, Photographer unknown, 1941, ATL, DA-02315-F; **p. 47:** Young Māori men cutting down a kauri tree in the Northland Region, Northwood Brothers, c.1910, ATL, 1/1-006263-G; **p. 48:** Unidentified man holding up large crayfish in Northland, Leo White, 1930, ATL, WA-25226-G; **p. 51:** Unidentified man, Whanganui district, Photographer unknown, Date unknown, ATL, 1/1-000049-G; **p. 52:** Sir Apirana Ngata taking the lead in a haka on Waitangi Day at the centennial celebrations at Waitangi, Bert Snowden, 1940, ATL, 1/2-029794-F; **p. 55:** Annual World War One Māori Servicemen's Reunion, Tikitiki marae, Ans Westra, 1963, AWM-0443-F_08; **p. 56:** Māori boy with a rugby ball, Waikato, Leo White, 1938, ATL, WA-12550-G; **p. 59:** Māori boy carrying a milk container, Waikato, Leo White, 1938, ATL, WA-12540-G; **p. 61:** Maori Battalion performing a haka for the King of Greece, Photographer unknown, 1941, ATL, DA-01231-F; **p. 62:** Members of the Maori Battalion in Greece, Photographer unknown, 1941, ATL, DA-01229-F; **p. 65:** Inner pā at the New Zealand International Exhibition, Christchurch, Leslie Hinge, 1906, ATL, 1/1-022026-G.

Atawhai – Compassion

p. 66: Mother and baby outside a marae, Leo White, 1930, ATL, WA-03182-G; **p. 69:** Māori boy crying, Leo White, 1938, ATL, WA-12543-G; **p. 70:** Māori Minister for Ratana Church, Taupo, Leo White, 1948, ATL, WA-12467-G; **p. 73:** Hei tiki on display, William Price, c.1910, ATL, 1/2-001919-G; **p. 74:** Tangi on the marae, Ngaruawahia, Ans Westra, 1962, AWM-0142-F_06; **p. 77:** Waipiro Bay, Gisborne, Ans Westra, 1963, AWM-0488-F_08; **p. 78:** Ruatoria (from *Washday at the Pā*), Ans Westra, 1963, AWM-0584-F_08; **p. 81:** Māori woman with catch of fish, Northland, Arthur Northwood, c.1910, ATL, 1/1-006322-G; **p. 82:** Mother with baby, Leo White, 1930, ATL, WA-03183-G; **p. 84:** Māori woman weaving flax, Leo White, 1948, ATL, WA-12494-G; **p. 87:** Two elderly Māori woman, Richard Northwood, c.1900, ATL, 1/1-005700b-G.

Ngākau Tapatahi – Integrity

p. 88: Sophia Hinerangi, William Partington, c.1900, ATL, 1/1-003104-G; **p. 91:** Ringatu meeting, Ruatoki, Ans Westra, 1963, AWM-0221-F_06; **p. 92:** Wellington Diocese Māori Anglican Hui Aroha, Masterton, Ans Westra, 1961, AWM-0360-F_06; **p. 95:** Parakino School, Whanganui River, Ans Westra, 1963, AWM-0403-F_11; **p. 96:** Sheep dipping, Adkin farm, Levin, George Adkin, 1906, ATL, 1/4-023364-G; **p. 99:** Māori wahine, Leo White, 1948, ATL, WA-12460-G; **p. 100:** Māori man wearing a korowai, William Partington, 1903, ATL, 10x12-0023-G; **p. 103:** Homestead, Wairarapa, Ans Westra, 1960, AWM-0118-F_08; **p. 104:** Painting the Waiwhetu marae, Lower Hutt, Ans Westra, 1960, AWM-0041-F_04; **p. 107:** Tangi on the marae, Ngaruawahia, Ans Westra, 1962, AWM-0142-F_08.

Whakahautanga – Self-mastery

p. 108: Before the game, *Evening Post* staff photographer, 1950, ATL, 114/181/03-G;
p. 111: Māori woman weaving a basket, Tourist & Publicity Department, Date unknown, ATL, 1/1-017331-F; **p. 112:** Sir Apirana Ngata, Earle Andrew, c.1940, ATL, 1/4-021044-F;
p. 115: Young boy crying in front of a vehicle, Leo White, 1938, ATL, WA-12545-G; **p. 116:** Men setting a crayfish pot, Frederick Hargreaves, ATL, 1/1-002601-G; **p. 118:** Māori man sorting kūmara, Arthur Northwood, c.1920, ATL, 1/1-006227-G; **p. 121:** Dining hall, Waiwhetu marae, Lower Hutt, Ans Westra, 1960, AWM-0060-2-F_03; **p. 122:** Rangiatea Anglican Māori Church, Otaki, Ans Westra, 1962, AWM-0350-F_01; **p. 125:** Outside Civic Library, Wellington, Ans Westra, 1960, AWM-0365-F_05; **p. 126:** Sergeant P. Walters, George Bull, 1943, ATL, DA-04138-F; **p. 129:** Two Māori boys net fishing, Waikato, Leo White, 1938, ATL, WA-12556-G.

Whakapono – Belief

p. 130: Māori woman in feather cloak, Leo White, 1938, ATL, WA-12588-F; **p. 133:** Hiruharama (Jerusalem), Whanganui River, Ans Westra, 1963, AWM-0268-F_05; **p. 135:** Māori boys holding kina, Thelma Kent, c.1939, ATL, 1/2-010198-F; **p. 136:** Hone Tuwhare at Kaka Point, Ans Westra, 1988; **p. 138:** Unknown man (possibly Anania Amohau), Tourist & Publicity Department, c.1945, ATL, 1/1-021397-F; **p. 141:** Rotorua, Ans Westra, 1963, AWM-0237-F_07;
p. 142: Pipiriki, Whanganui River, Ans Westra, 1963, AWM-0267-F_02; **p. 145:** Londa, Whakarewarewa, Ans Westra, 1963, AWM-0228-F_03; **p. 146:** A young Māori woman wearing a korowai, James McDonald, c.1900, Te Papa Tongarewa, C.025062; **p. 149:** Ruatoria with Mount Hikurangi in the distance, Leo White, 1953, ATL, WA-32825-F; **p. 151:** Māori man in feather cloak, Leo White, 1938, ATL, WA-12602-G; **p. 152:** Rangiatea Anglican Māori Church, Otaki, Ans Westra, 1962, AWM-0350-F_01; **p. 155:** Waiwhetu marae, Lower Hutt, Ans Westra, 1960, AWM-0882-F_03; **pp. 156–57:** Māori boys and an Indian boy walking down the road, Waikato, Leo White, 1938, ATL, WA-12555-G.